Reading Toward Success

Reading Toward Success

Tried-and-True Reading Practices for Raising Successful Kids

Rachael T. Reiton

Reiton Publishing ◊ Winthrop, MA

Published in Winthrop, Massachusetts, by Reiton Publishing

www.reitonpublishing.com

Discounted bulk orders for school districts can be requested from the publisher at: reitonpublishing@gmail.com or 63 Ingleside Ave., Winthrop, MA 02152.

ISBN (ebook) 978-0-9988575-4-1

ISBN (paperback) 978-0-9988575-5-8

Book cover design by dalim of 99designs.com

Cover artwork created by Freepik

Front cover font is Dimbo, created by Jayvee D. Enaguas (Grand Chaos), © 2009, 2010, 2011, 2012 GrandChaos9000. Some Rights Reserved. (Under Licensed by Creative Commons CC-BY-SA 3.0) https://creativecommons.org/licenses/by-sa/3.0/

For my parents, to whom I owe everything

Contents

The Story Behind This Book

I want to begin this book by being absolutely and completely honest with you about who I am and why I've written this book.

When I decided to become a reading teacher at the age of 24, I had zero—and I mean *zero*—experience in teaching anything except Sunday school. I was working at a high-end stationery store in Chicago with a bachelor's degree in communications under my belt, but I knew sales wasn't going to be a career for me. My friends told me that I would make a good teacher, and so I decided to go back to school to get my second B.A. in secondary education.

My choice of subject matter to teach? Reading.

Why? Well, because I loved to read...

And that was about as far as my passion for reading went. It went as far as me.

Fast forward 16 years. My career had morphed from sixth-grade reading teacher into middle school reading-lab instructor into elementary and middle school librarian—with a few years thrown in for additional schooling, substitute teaching and waitressing as I pursued my library certification. During those 16 years I taught and mentored kids from both urban

Chicagoland and rural Wisconsin, from all walks of life, and falling anywhere in age between third and eighth grade.

By now it was the end of my thirteenth year of teaching–and I found myself at a major fork in the road. Not only was I preparing to send my stepson off to college but also for my husband and I to move halfway across the country to Boston. In the midst of the emotional and psychological strain of it all, I did a lot of thinking about my next career move. Loving my work with books but frustrated with the public school system, I decided to take this large fork in life's road and dive into the career that had been pent up inside of me my entire life: writing.

And so here I am.

How would I describe my passion for reading *now*, you may ask?

Honestly, I feel more on fire than I've ever been about teaching reading and for two very different, fiery reasons.

One fire in my heart is burning because my years of working with kids had an effect I never expected back when I started my teaching degree: they took my love for reading and turned it into a love for *teaching* reading.

The second flame, almost as bright, was lit during my final years working as a school librarian. The more time I gave to my teaching career, the more I witnessed, year after year, additional "curriculum" being added to teachers' plates by government and school administrations–until the amount of time children spent reading in the classroom every week was tragically low.

Not only that, I experienced my job as a librarian (or "library media specialist") change from being a promoter and propounder of books and reading to being a keyboarding and technology teacher.

My title and position change weren't unique in any sense of the word. A large portion of the nation's public schools were headed in the same direction. It's the reason why I still can't return to teaching in public schools: my passion has a difficult time working within the system as it stands.

In my opinion, this shift away from reading is leaving kids high and dry. The rabid pursuit of technology education in schools is forcing out *the* most important skill any of our kids can learn and largely replacing it with class time learning how to use apps and how to be respectful to people online.

I'm sorry if I am coming across as sardonic, but a nerve in me has been touched—a nerve that after 13 years of reading with kids has become extremely sensitive. I've seen what reading does to kids. I've seen what technology does to kids. And I tell you from my soapbox: *what technology does for kids does not even BEGIN to compare with the life-changing effects of reading.*

Learning how to use apps is something that kids do on their own. And as for teaching kids how to be respectful to others? That's *our* job as parents. Period.

Reading—unlike technology, no matter what the rest of the world may tell you—is not only the cornerstone from which all other learning is built upon. It is the foundation of learning and discovering who we are as individuals. It is the skill that is necessary to become independent learners and vital in guiding our self-discovery. Reading gives us the skills to become critical thinkers, furthers our understanding of others, and increases our knowledge of the world around us. Reading is the gateway to true independence and success in life.

This is my heartfelt belief, and this is why I have written this book.

Thirteen years in the public school system have taught me that—at least at the moment, with the system's steady progression away from a reading-based curriculum—schools are no longer going to provide the amount of help parents might be used to and need when it comes to reading. And, unfortunately, when schools do teach reading, the systems tend to have teachers implement the latest educational fad which most parents tend not to be familiar with.

In my experience, most parents (and teachers!) want what is tried-and-true for their children—not the latest fad—and when it comes to reading, folks, I'm right there with you!

So where does this leave us?

It leaves us with YOU as the primary educator, role model and advocate of reading for your child.

But I'm not a reader! you say. *There's NO way that I can be a reading role model for my child and help her (or him) become a successful reader!*

That is where this little book comes in: because you CAN.

I know that parents panic at the thought of helping their kids become better readers, but it's not what you think. You *can* help your child learn to read and *love* to read, and I'm going to share with you the techniques I personally used with your own kids throughout my career. (Which brings me to a point: all student names have been changed in this book.)

Use this book like a guidebook. Mark it up, highlight, take notes. Make use of the resources and reading lists I include at the end of the book.

I promise I am not going to hand you statistics or fads that will change from one day to the next, nor will I give you tricks to "magically" make your child a better reader. What I *will* do is provide simple steps or "practices" that I used in my classroom and in my libraries—basic procedures that transformed children who hated to read into kids who loved to read. How? The kids saw the value in what reading and sharing great books did to their hearts and minds.

Learning to read changes us, you see. I sincerely believe that you as a parent hold immense power to your child's success if you understand reading's importance and work to strengthen it in your child. You—more than any teacher, book fair or reading program—can be the one who teaches your child the vital skills needed to become successful in reading and, ultimately, in life.

So read on! I promise it's simple. And who knows? You may just find yourself becoming more successful along the way, too.

Practice #1: Understand What It Means to "Know How to Read"

I don't know how many times it happened to me: I would be involved in a casual conversation with someone I had just met. We would begin with the cursory weather, then move onto something like where each other lived, and then the inevitable question would roll around: "So, what do you do?"

Upon learning that I was a reading teacher, my partner in dialogue would more often than not exclaim, "Oh, my granddaughter [or daughter, niece, etc.]! She just *loves* books! She is such a smart little thing! She's only three years old, and she already knows how to read!"

Every time I would bite my tongue, but in my head I was thinking: "*No, she doesn't. Not really.*"

Many of us have the understanding that to be able to read means that I can look at a series of letters strung together (i.e. a word) and say them out loud, using the correct pronunciation, of course.

Well, that's a start. But there is much more to reading than being able to sound out or sight-read a word.

If there is one thing that I want you to remember about "knowing how to read," it is this:

Reading = Understanding

Reading is not being able to sound out a word. Reading is not being able to parrot back a story that has been heard numerous times. Reading is not even being able to stumble through a string of words that make up a sentence.

Reading is being able to *understand* what those strings of words mean when put together as a sentence and, ultimately, being able to further understand a group of sentences, comprehending their meaning as they work together to produce a more complex thought or idea.

When I first began teaching my students how to write, I quickly realized that I could not teach them how to write a sentence without simultaneously teaching them grammar through diagramming. To start the process, I would put a "sentence" up on the overhead, showing a long string of letters, and ask the kids to read it.

"We can't!" they'd say.

"Why not?" I'd ask.

"Because you need to put spaces to make words!"

So I'd put up the same string with spaces between groups of letters. "No!" the kids hollered. "Those aren't words! They don't mean anything!"

So I'd change the groups of letters to make real words but in a random order. "No!" Fists would shake in the air. "You have to put the words in order! The words have to make sense! That order doesn't mean anything!'

AH HA!!!! They got it!

And *that* is what it means to "know how to read." Words have meaning, whether we are writing them or reading them, and when we are able to understand them, *then* we have learned the most beautiful and important of life skills: we have learned to read.

Is this reading an easy thing to learn how to do?

Heck, no. That's why it used to be focused on so intensely in school. Remember "The Three Rs?" **R**eading. '**R**iting. '**R**ithmetic. The three essential cores of knowledge that are truly necessary to master in order to become independent in life.

That learned independence is why it is so important that you become heavily involved in helping your child understand and learn how to read and to read well.

Nervous? Don't be. That's why I'm here. Let me walk you through the next practice of what you can do to help. It's super simple, I promise.

Practice #2: Keep a Bookshelf

I know I'm not the only one who finds it a bit mesmerizing and magical to stand and stare at a bookshelf full of books. Anytime I walk into a library or a bookstore I find it difficult to look at all those books and not wonder what each one is all about. What do they say? What stories do they tell?

Then there is the artwork on the covers. The intriguing titles. And the sizes! Big, fat, heavy books. Tall books. Tiny books. Light, toss-in-my-bag paperback books.

And what do all those shelves full of books make us do? You know how it is! They make us curious, and we all reach out and...pull one off the shelf! We can't keep our hands to ourselves. The books beg to be picked up, handled, flipped through, perused.

When I was a middle school librarian, one of my summer goals was to have a whole section of new books ready and waiting for that first day of school. As the kids walked into the library during their Day 1 tour, it was inevitable: all eyes and hands went directly to those brand new, never-before-seen books, the covers calling with their bright colors and eye-catching fonts, those untold stories waiting to be discovered. Kids fought over who got to check out which books first. Waiting lists grew. I was begged to send emails to "whoever has that book checked out because they've had it for a month, and I want it!"

The excitement kids had when they finally got that book can be duplicated in your very own home. All it takes is coming up with a bookshelf and then filling it with tantalizing books. The size, location and construction of your bookshelf are entirely up to you, but here are some ideas to get you started.

THE SIZE

If you are a new parent looking to start your child's collection or if you are someone who is looking to set up your very first bookshelf, start small. A two-shelfer will do, but feel free to go smaller. Even a single, wall-mounted shelf will work just fine to organize your budding collection.

If you are setting up a bookshelf for picture books, a single shelf may suffice. Those of you looking at early chapter books or books for young adults may need to plan on having more room sooner rather than later. Kids starting grade school seem to be attracted to series books, and the number of books in some series can be quite large! And the older kids get, the thicker the books tend to get, so make sure you give your bookshelf some growing room. You may need to rotate some books off the shelf if you are really limited on space, but remember to keep those favorites within reach!

What's important here is to have a full shelf that includes a number of books your child *hasn't* read. Always provide access to a selection of unread stories. It helps keeps the mystery of reading alive. Kids used to walk into the library and, staring at all the full shelves, ask me with awe, "Have you *read* all of these books?"

"No," I would tell them with a smile. "Not yet."

Make that forever be your child's goal. Always have that one book that is still waiting... That way there is *always* something to read.

THE LOCATION

Where the bookshelf is located is going to be partly dictated by other important factors discussed in the next few chapters: *where* and *when* the reading will primarily take place. Obviously you will want to encourage reading wherever your child goes, but it is important to provide a specific place at home that triggers the reaction of: "*Oooh, that's my reading spot. I want to go read...*" Place your bookshelf near this location.

You also will want to consider your child's height. Do you have a little one? Put the bookshelf down low for easy access. Have a sprouting teenage girl or boy? Put those books at eye-level, baby! Pique, tantalize and feed that exploding imagination.

As your collection grows larger and larger (we will talk about how to grow it in a bit), bookshelves can be added to additional rooms. I personally have bookshelves all over my house. The books in each room tend to match what kinds of activities are done or the topics of discussions we tend to have in that room: cookbooks in the kitchen. Classics in the dining room. Narrative non-fiction and fiction in the den. History, art and poetry in the living room. Hobbies, travel and how-tos in the family room.

Building collections of all sorts of books teaches kids that reading is used *all the time* in order to learn about and appreciate EVERYTHING. I still love the work of an animal portraitist named Robert Bateman and remember the chilling sun worship rituals of Native Americans pictured in books my dad had shelved next to the record player. I'd sit with giant headphones on, listening to my records and reading those books all afternoon.

CONSTRUCTION

What your bookshelf is made of is, once again, entirely up to you. Do not think you need to go spend hundreds of dollars on a giant, solid wood bookshelf. My parents made our bookshelf out of cinder blocks and wood boards when I was a kid. It worked. In fact, they still use it.

Pinterest contains hundreds of creative book storage ideas and ways to create your own bookshelves. Check out my board, "Bookshelf Ideas," to get an idea of just a few (username is *Reiton Publishing*).

Do you like the idea of displaying books bookstore-style, cover facing out as a hint of what's inside? Go with a simple ledge, adding more ledges to the wall as your collection grows. Not sure what to use as a ledge? Make your own from wooden brackets and 1"x4"s from the hardware store.

If you are familiar with a sewing machine (or sewing by hand!), hem two sides of a piece of fabric and sling it between two dowel rods hung on double-brackets. Attach the brackets to the wall or even to the side of a dresser.

Want more of a library feel? File your books on a shelf, spine facing outward, but get creative with that shelf! Stack together wooden crates. Or remove drawers from an old dresser and paint the empty spaces a vibrant color as backdrop for your books. How about just lining the wall with sturdy baskets tipped on their sides?

Or use those baskets as they were intended and have baskets of books instead of shelves. Not only do they make the books easy to move, they allow them to be tucked into a corner if you are more limited on space.

But—*what about ebooks?* you ask.

Ebooks certainly have their time and place. They are great for easily taking a "stack" of books when traveling or for trying out a free sample chapter of a book before buying. They can also be quite useful with their "touch-a-word-to-look-up-its-definition" feature when you are reading a book with a lot of unknown words.

But when it comes to building a home library, a physical book literally puts one in a different mental state with its very tactile and physical presence. Holding a book, sensing the progress through the story,—heck, *smelling* the pages... It just doesn't compare with an ebook. (And if you don't know the smell I'm talking about, go stick your nose in an older book. Really.)

The main idea when setting up your bookshelf is to entice. Create a display of books that draws attention, is easily accessed by your child, and—as we will discuss next—is close at hand to what will become your child's favorite place: the comfy chair.

Practice #3: Provide a Comfy Chair

It was late in the summer when I toured the two libraries I would be maintaining as the new school librarian. One was at the district's elementary school and one at the middle school. I remember being shocked as my new principals led me around my new work spaces. How crowded, boring and unwelcoming the libraries were! Both libraries were crammed with wobbly tables and stiff, straight-backed chairs whose upholstery was stained and worn. The elementary school was outfitted with an enormous carousel of computers. The middle school was overcrowded with embarrassingly outdated books and, therefore, too many bookshelves and rickety spinners. Neither library was a comfortable space to work or read, so, not surprisingly when my school year started, the kids never came to the library.

Thank heavens for supportive principals and an aide with muscles of steel who quickly understood our need to provide a relaxing, inviting place for the kids to work. In the middle school, this meant moving out a lot of those rickety tables and horrid wooden chairs and bringing in a few donated (i.e. vintage) sofas and a coffee table or two from Goodwill. In the elementary school my aide and I moved the computers and the monstrous carousel out of the library and brought in what became known as "the comfy chairs:" inexpensive, leather club chairs and ottomans found online, which we interspersed with some (also donated) reading lights.

You wouldn't believe how the library environments changed after those simple modifications. The middle schoolers suddenly were requesting to come to the library just to lie on the couch and read. Teachers started using the space as a reward to their students for being productive and completing assignments.

At the elementary school, where I had structured class times, the kids would beg me to have a "Reading Day." Instead of teaching my information literacy curriculum, I would project a fake fireplace on the whiteboard, turn out most of the lights, turn on a Beethoven CD, and allow the kids to sit or lie wherever they wished in the library to read their books. We had to make a revolving list of who got the "comfy chairs" so the kids wouldn't fight over them.

Not a single kid ever complained about those "Reading Days"—not even the kids who weren't "good readers." Every student found their own cozy spot and for half an hour read a book or two (okay, someone always tried to talk to a friend, but once moved, they read!).

My students reminded me that part of what makes reading so enjoyable is having that special place to do it: a place that is physically comfortable, inviting and specifically used *just* for reading.

MAKE IT COMFY

As my students demonstrated with their weekly arguments,

everyone wants something cozy to curl up and read in (or on). What determines "cozy" will depend on your child. If you are a new parent, that means *you* will be the cozy spot. Put a rocker or a glider in your child's nursery for *your* comfort and then your lap and the soothing motion will provide that cozy spot for your baby as you read.

If your child is older, you've got more options. You may even want to have a talk with your child about what they want. Would they prefer an overstuffed reading chair? A pile of pillows? A porch swing? Grandma's old sofa? Let them choose from a range of options. If you don't have something around the house to use and can't afford something new, here's a tip: take a look at resale and thrift shops. I think the most expensive reading chair I've bought from a church thrift store was $15; the cheapest was $5!

You also might want to consider having a stuffed animal "friend," a throw pillow or a blanket at hand. You want your child to curl up with that book like they are best friends—and best friends typically don't sit stiffly next to each other. They get close.

MAKE IT INVITING AND DISTRACTION-FREE

I'm not going to delve into the psychology of it all, but the most special reading spots tend to be out-of-the-way. They are called "reading nooks" for a reason. Look around your house and think about where your child would enjoy reading. It might simply be their bedroom. But do you have any other cool places that could become a little reading haven? A cubby or closet you could clear out? A hidden attic corner? An old couch curtained off in the basement?

It isn't critical that you find an unused corner in order to create a good reading spot. Space might necessitate it be your living room. What's important is that the location is distraction-free, even if momentarily—allowing your child to get lost in the world of their imagination. This means removing or turning off noises and objects such as phones, TVs, gaming systems and stereos. It might even mean removing other children who are not reading. Create a space that allows your child to completely forget everything around them.

Lighting is an important part of making that space inviting. Have a shaded reading lamp that casts warm light downward onto the book. Avoid Edison bulbs; they don't cast a strong enough light to read by. Keep the bulb within the 40-60 watt range if incandescent or 10-15 watts if LED (these translate to 600-900 lumens). Even if the location is by a window, provide a lamp. Reading is an especially wonderful escape on those rainy days when the light shining through the windows isn't that great. That warm glow will help illuminate the pages and set the cozy mood.

MAKE IT SACRED

Now that you've got your child's "cozy spot" set up, do your best to make that spot totally sacred. It should be the place where nothing else exists except your child and their book, and nothing else happens except reading, even if just for that designated span of "reading time." Period.

Be forewarned that your child's cozy reading spot may change over time. We had lots of random nooks and crannies built into the house where I grew up. I think every single one of them became a reading nook for me at some point. I even went through a stretch as a middle-schooler where I loved to climb a specific tree in my backyard and settle onto a particular branch and read for an hour after school. There I would hide, sheltered in the leafy green glow, completely lost in another world with no sense of the here-and-now.

That's what reading does to us: it gets us lost in time. And that leads us to our next important practice: time.

Practice #4: Make Time Every Single Day

So we've talked about getting your child prepared to read by setting up both a bookshelf full of books and a cozy place for him or her to take one of those books and get lost in their imaginary world. Now we need to get down to the brass tacks and talk about reading itself. But first, a story...

Up until I was about three years old, the Saturday morning ritual for me and my two sisters was to wake up before our parents did, shuffle to the living room, and hunker down on the shag carpet to watch *Sesame Street*. It's a ritual that probably would have continued for a long, long time if it were not for the following event.

While we were watching Big Bird, Oscar the Grouch and Grover one fine morning, there was a sudden blinding flash, a popping sound—and the television screen went blank.

The TV was dead. Like, dead-dead.

Little did we kids know but my parents talked long and hard together about replacing that television. It wasn't just the financial expense. It was the time expense, too. My father realized that watching sports had been taking up an awful lot of his time at home. And my mother found that she didn't miss the news like she thought she would—nor the constant noise she had previously filled her quiet house with, much of the time while not even actively watching TV.

And we kids? Well, being kids, we very quickly found ways to fill the now vacant Saturday mornings. My eldest sister took to lazily reading in bed, and that—that was the final straw. My parents decided: no more TV. It was going to be books and our imaginations for all of us from now on.

You see, one thing that is absolutely vital to understand about reading is this: **reading is a skill**. It is not something that some people are just naturally "good at" and others aren't. Skills are *learned*, and learning means WORK.

So, if reading is a skill, this means:

1. Reading needs to be practiced.
2. Our different brains are going to learn how to read in different ways.
3. If we stop reading, our skills become rusty.

Let's take a look at how each of these facts play themselves out.

READING MUST BE PRACTICED TO BE MASTERED

Reading is a type of brain exercise, and like any other skill or exercise—pitching a baseball, playing the piano, walking a tightrope—reading cannot be mastered unless it is practiced. Absolutely, positively can NOT.

Just as with practicing baseball or piano or the tightrope, if you practice a few times a week, you'll get pretty good. If you *never* practice? Well...you'll be quite the opposite.

But if you devote time to practice every single day?

You will become *great*. Guaranteed!

As discussed earlier, being a good reader does not mean that you can sit and read sentence after sentence without making a stumbling mistake or mispronunciation. There are people who can read page after page with perfect enunciation and clarity, and they don't understand a single thing they've read.

Being a good reader means you can look at a string of words and pronounce them correctly AND, even more importantly, that you *understand* the meaning of that string of words.

And the coolest thing is this: when you get *really* good at reading, you start learning that there can be more than one way to interpret what someone wrote. I used to give an example of this to my kids:

"Pretend I get a new pair of shoes," I'd say to them, "and I wear them to school the next day. In the morning I see you, and I say to you, 'Check out my new pair of shoes! Do you like them?'

"And you respond, 'Yeahhhhhhhhhhh...'

"Tell me," I'd ask the kids. "Do you really like my shoes?"

"No," they'd say. "I said I did, but the *way* I said it shows that I don't."

Being a good reader is understanding what the words in a story mean, and getting to that point takes a lot of practice. But when you learn to see and understand the multiple layers of meaning in a story (i.e. I *said* that I liked your shoes because I'm a kind person and I didn't want to hurt your feelings, but how I said it really *showed* that I didn't like them)–THAT is being a master reader. But it takes lots of exercise for your brain to get there. You have GOT to practice every single day!

OUR BRAINS ARE DIFFERENT

Another important thing to remember about learning to read is this: how your child learns may be entirely different from the way the child next door or the "smart" kid in class or *you* learn. How each of our brains wires itself is based on so many things: our genes, our environment, our life experiences, the knowledge we've already gained, our learning style.

Because our brains are wired differently, we learn differently.

Why am I bringing this up? Because I don't want you to worry if your child struggles to learn to read! If a learning disability comes into play, don't sweat it. I've worked with many different kids who have had various disabilities: autism, dyslexia, language barriers, or simply being "behind" others in their grade.

What I've learned (and tried to instill in my students) is this: learning to read is *not* a race. Someone is not necessarily a "good reader" if they are the first or fastest reader in the class. Here's the test: when your child is asked questions that require understanding some of the complexities of the story, is he or she able to answer them? Remember: reading requires not just that you can say a word or can spout back something that happens in a story. It requires that you *understand* the meaning and can make connections *within* the story.

It's okay if your child's brain takes longer to learn to read. It's okay if your child reads at a slower pace. Folks, I will tell you this: it was not unusual for some of my students in the "lower-level" reading classes to make more powerful connections in a story than any of my "higher-level" students did. It just may be their pace was slower because the connections they were forming were deeper.

WANT TO GET RUSTY?

How the human brain makes these connections is a remarkable thing. Here is what happens in a very simplified nutshell: the brain loves to learn so much that brain cells (neurons) literally reach and grow towards each other like little hands as your brain is learning a new skill. Every time you practice your new skill, no matter how many mistakes you make, those neurons grow and reach towards each other. Mistakes are part of the learning! And when you finally do master that skill—you know what? (This is so cool!) Those cells actually *become* interconnected. Those little "hands" of the brain cells clasp together.

To help my younger students remember how the brain works, I used to have the kids hold their hands apart with their fingers spread, and then as I would talk about practicing and practicing, the kids would move their hands closer and closer together. And when I would ask, "What happens when we've finally got it?" (meaning they'd learned the skill), the kids would clasp their hands together into a ball.

Then I would ask them this: "What happens when we stop practicing? No matter *how good* we are?" And their little hands would slowly pull apart until the connection was broken.

Reading is a skill that needs continual practice, no matter how good of a reader you are, no matter how long you've been reading. If you don't read, you get rusty. Guaranteed.

Time must be set aside every day for your child (and you!) to read. Ultimately, it doesn't matter when. It just matters that it happens. Daily reading, even if it is just 10 or 15 minutes, will make those brain connections stronger and stronger, turning your child into a stronger and stronger reader.

You as the parent will have a pretty good idea of when "reading time" should be, but make your child part of that conversation. When does he or she think is the best time? Should it be during homework time? Or should it be removed from a "work" mindset and be built into the morning routine? Or an after-school, "before-you-start-your-homework" break? What about being "dessert" after dinner and serving it up with cookies and milk? Or how about bath time? Bed time? Somewhere in between?

Again, it doesn't matter when. It only matters that it happens. I will go so far as to say that this reading brain exercise should be priority number one on your list, tied for first place only with providing the body what it physically needs: exercise, a healthy diet and plenty of solid rest.

Make it happen. Make time for your child to read *every single day*.

Need some ideas on how to do that? The next practice is going to show you exactly how: by doing it TOGETHER.

Practice #5: Read Together

When it comes to helping your child become a successful reader, a particular saying comes to mind: "*Practice what you preach.*"

We all need to be reminded from time to time that we as parents are *the* most influential role model our kids will ever have. Who our children become depends largely on who WE are and what behaviors we practice and act out for them to re-enact in turn.

Reading is one of those fundamental practices.

I understand that most of us know how to read. But many of us don't read well because we don't practice. Not practicing makes us think we don't like to read, and then we do a terrible, horrible thing: we *tell* our kids we don't like to read.

I will never advocate lying to your child, and maybe you really *don't* like to read, but *showing* your child that you read is hugely important. You are their role model, so it's time to start. And that doesn't mean faking it by having a huge stack of books on your bedside table that you never touch. It means *actually* reading out loud with your child. And I'm not just talking when they are babies and toddlers, either. I mean when they are in grade school. Middle school. High school.

"Say WHAT?" I can hear you now. "Read together with my *middle schooler*??? I'm the world's biggest embarrassment to my child right now, and you want me to READ OUT LOUD with him?"

Believe me, I get it. I didn't read with my middle schooler, either. But I wish I had. I really, *really* regret that I didn't find it important enough to make time to read and "talk books" with my stepson, Michael.

Why? What *are* the benefits of reading with our kids at *all* ages? Let's take a look.

READING WITH INFANTS AND TODDLERS

The first night my sister and her husband brought William home from the hospital, my brother-in-law held the tiny guy in his arms and read my nephew a bedtime story. The next night, they did it again. And the next, again.

Years later—no matter how far past his bedtime it might be—William curls up with his mom or dad (or me, if I'm visiting!) and reads at least two books.

What are his parents instilling?

Well, first off: a routine. Reading has become part of William's daily schedule, and his day is not complete without it. In fact, my sister tells me he *insists* that he gets his reading time before he goes to bed (and I'm sure that is the one and only thing my sister allows him to insist upon!).

Secondly, William's parents are showing that reading is *important*. Important enough that even if you are going to bed past your bedtime, reading needs to happen every single day.

Finally, William's parents are building the habit of reading *together*. William will never know any different. It will be perfectly normal for his mom or his dad to sit with him and read because it has happened for as long as he can remember. That is—as long as they stick with it.

READING WITH PRIMARY AND ELEMENTARY SCHOOL KIDS

When children begin attending school, their desire to read suddenly grows exponentially. With every new letter they learn, with every new word they know how to write and pronounce, their longing to read skyrockets—as long as the desire is fed.

As we discussed previously, the only way for your child to get better and better at reading is to actually read! I cannot stress it enough: take this amazing desire that every child is given, help them latch onto it, and then feed it. In addition to reading the books you have on your bookshelf and the books your child brings home from school, go to the library as often as possible and checkout stacks, heaps, *piles* of books. Then go home, sit down and read, read, read with your child. Wherever. Whenever. READ TOGETHER.

Something very important to note: at this stage of life, kids are sponges. They soak up everything, and they have an almost insatiable capacity to learn (sometimes to a point of exhaustion for us as parents!). Use this hunger to your advantage by practicing the following when you read together at home:

- Read slowly.
- Demonstrate how to sound-out words. (Remember the purple Two-Headed Monster that sat behind the wall on *Sesame Street*? Do it like that.)

- For simply worded books, use your finger to follow along and point to words as you say them. As your child becomes a better reader, follow the sentences with your finger.
- Obey punctuation! Stop at periods. Emphasize the exclamation points! Raise your tone at question marks. Avoid being monotone!
- Use expression and feeling when you read. Think about what is being said, and make your voice show the emotion.
- Do voices. Do accents! Remember: this is the age where kids think that you are the coolest and that everything you do is totally awesome, so take advantage and let loose!

Your child will learn all of these skills from *your* example, and then one day–your child is going to read to *you*.

Yes! It will be a glorious day! Celebrate!

But DON'T STOP READING TOGETHER.

READING WITH MIDDLE AND HIGH SCHOOL KIDS

This is where the panic sets in. I get it. Really, I do. I remember "The Shift." Within a matter of days you go from being treated like the coolest person in the world to being the most embarrassing and annoying. Instead of being sought out, you are avoided–*especially* if friends are in sight. And when young adults are with their friends, most of them *think* they want to avoid you like the plague.

But when they are at home, kids are still kids and still really *do* want to be shown love and attention. Reading together with your child provides the opportunity to do both. Continue the habit of reading together, and–may I promise you something?

Your participation in their reading will not only continue to help your child develop their reading skills but also their communication and social skills.

I've step-parented through the middle school and high school stages, so I know this time of life can get really awkward and busy. I also know that we all come from an infinite number of walks-of-life. Some of you are single parents. Some of you work four jobs. Some of you have schedules that make it difficult to even spend time with your kids. I wish I could magically make it easy for all of you to find time to read with your kids. The reality is: it's going to be difficult for some of you, and I am sorry for that. But remember: we are talking about fine-tuning a skill that is vital to your child's independence for the rest of their life. You MUST find time to read together. Even if it's 10 minutes. If anything, *now* is the time to be emphasizing to your child the importance of making time to read despite a busy schedule, because, as we all know, life doesn't slow down after high school.

Here are some thoughts to help ease the dread of reading with your middle or high schooler and just possibly encourage you to get started right away:

- The young adult novels written nowadays (called 'YA' by the hip crowd, just an FYI...) are quite good. Some are actually downright fantastic. Lots of adults who don't have teenagers at home read them. Really.
- Your teenager will probably bring home a book that you read in high school. You will be amazed at how much better you understand the book now as an adult–and how capable you are at guiding your child's thoughts as you read the book together (more on this topic in the next

chapter).

- If you child isn't currently reading a particular book for school that you can read together at home, choose one together that you both want to read, and enjoy reading it just for fun.
- Take turns reading out loud. And if you need to start buying or checking out multiple copies of books from the library so you can each have one to hold and read along from, do it.
- Try splitting up the parts of the narration as well as the different characters' lines. Or, you read one page, your child reads the next. And dramatize those voices! Have fun with your reading together.

As a parent, I was a battle axe about my stepson getting enough rest. So if you can only read for 10-15 minutes before going to bed because the day has been insane, that's okay. The point is made to your child that you both are making time for two very important things: each other and reading.

Some of you will start this reading-together process from the cradle. Some of you will start it from high school. Regardless of when you begin, be persistent with your child about your time together. They may fight it at first, but you keep calmly and lovingly fighting back. They will cave eventually—because they secretly want to.

I heard a story of a mother who told her young teenaged daughter that she wanted to read with her. The daughter resisted, but the mother insisted. She bought a copy of the book her daughter was reading and started reading it with her, just as we've talked about. What amazed me about this story—and what shows the power of a parent's involvement—is when the daughter went off to *college*, she came home for break and told her mother that she still wanted the two of them to read together.

How's that for teaching a skill? And the teacher isn't the one who instilled that drive.

The mom did.

Let's read on to see what else you are capable of doing—just by talking.

Practice #6: Talk About It

As a reading teacher and a librarian, my absolute favorite part of getting the right book into the hands of the right kid was listening to their insatiable urge to talk about it.

I will never forget Jonathon walking into the library with a book in his hand. Jonathon was an eighth grader who I had known for several years. The book he was holding was *Always Running: La Vida Loca: Gang Days in L.A.* by Luis J. Rodriguez, a former L.A. gang member. I had bought the book specifically with Jonathon and his growing interest in gangs in mind.

Jonathon placed the book on the counter, looked me in the eyes and said to me, "This book changed my life."

Chills? Heck, yeah.

Jonathon and I then carried on a 15-minute conversation of what the book meant to him, he sharing how it impacted his very soul. Yes, I caused him to be late to class, but I believed this conversation to be so much more important than anything else in the long run.

Another student, Alex—a middle schooler who reportedly hated reading—walked into the library a few weeks after I had convinced him to read *To Kill a Mockingbird* (I told him it was one of my Top 5 and swore he would love it). He slid the book across the counter towards me and said, "Chapter 29." He shook his head. "Totally made me cry."

Am I serious??? Yes. I am.

A great story—whether true or fictitious—infects us with a fever because we connect with it in some meaningful way. The connection we feel is so strong that we find we must share the story with someone else. This is how most books wind up on the best-seller lists. How legends are born. Why you hear your kids telling the same dumb jokes that your grandpa told you. We instinctively want to talk about stories (or jokes) that we connect with—especially with someone whom we trust.

As you and your child read together, you are going to see this happen to the two of you, I promise. It will take some initiating on your part, but once you start guiding the questions and thought process, you are going to build a habit of not just reading books together but conversing about them, too.

One of the most fascinating things about reading books together with your child is this: because you and your child are two different people with two different lives, you will each have a different understanding of the stories that you read together.

I used to stress this truth to my students: the beauty of reading a book together and *talking* about it together is that we teach each other as we talk. *You* may pick up something in the story that doesn't stand out to me because *you* have experienced X-Y-Z, and I haven't. You have a chance to teach me a truth about the story—and probably about life—that I may never learn otherwise.

This wonderful reality is going to create opportunities for you and your child to discuss many things about a book. Let's look at three types of connections you can talk about: the story itself, the story and you, and the story and the real world.

I know it sounds obvious, but sometimes we adults just assume kids understand what's going on in a story because *we* get it. But adults have years of life experience and reading practice which help shape our ability to interpret what is taking place in a story. Kids don't have that background. They are more likely to take a story at face value and not really understand that there can be layers of backstory, emotions and what-ifs going on within the story.

You as the adult can help guide your child in thinking about the many different layers in the story—from the factual information that your child readily picks up on to the subtle hints in the story that aren't so obvious. Your regular guidance as you read together and talk about the story will teach your child how to think about the story from different angles—a critical skill to becoming a good reader.

Now here's the truth: when you are new to this whole "reading together" thing, you may struggle with coming up with topics or questions to talk about in regards to the story. You may at first find yourself simply asking your child questions about the facts of what is going on: Is the little boy happy or sad? What is the grandma baking? Who blew down the little pig's house?

This is a good starting point. It is important for anyone to remember the concrete elements that make up a story. You can't retell a story if you can't even remember the characters' names.

However, you are going to want to move on from just the fact-based "bones" of the story and get to the meat. A good story is more than just a bunch of strung-together facts. What makes a story a STORY is that "stuff" happens, and the characters feel strongly about this "stuff" that happens, and they respond to this "stuff" in ways that are good or bad or sometimes ugly!

Suddenly, there's a ton to talk about.

I used to tell my students: imagine that a story is the dirt in a garden and from it grows all kinds of things: the characters, the plot, the themes. But the story isn't just about what I see on the surface. There is a lot going on underneath the surface. My job as a good reader is to dig and find out what is going on under there. Why are characters acting a particular way? What is the reason the bad guy is a bad guy? Who is trustworthy in the story and who isn't? How will the main character solve this huge problem? What is the huge problem in the story, anyway?

Do you see how that works? Those big 'W' question words (who, what, where, when, why—and how) really help steer your child how to think about what's going on in the story.

When it comes to children's books and graphic novels, don't forget to look at the pictures. The pictures are there to help tell the story, too. Great illustrators are very good at creating a visual world that supports the text but may not be directly stated in the story. In picture books, look for details in the illustrations. What do they show is happening in the story? How is the story being told by the pictures? You will be amazed at how much the illustrations add to the story when you really start looking.

I also encourage you: even as your child gets older and you are reading novels together, reread a book together. One year my reading lab students asked if we could reread the book *Feathers* by Jacqueline Woodson, a book that we had read together the previous year. It was a wonderful experience listening to the kids talk about how much more they understood during their second reading. Even though they "knew" the story, they were able to see the story in a whole new, deeper light *because* they knew what was going to happen. Always leave that option open to you and your child.

TALK ABOUT THE STORY AND YOU

Once you and your child are comfortable talking about all the fascinating layers of the book, you can begin introducing thoughts that step outside the story and start relating the story to—YOU.

Yes, *you*. As I said before, your life experience will cause you to interpret a story differently than your child will. You have lived through events that have shaped you into who you are. You have changed your behavior because of the relationships you have had with others. You have learned lessons your child has not. You have a lot to bring to the discussion when you start making personal connections to a story. And your child is going to love hearing about it. Guaranteed.

And do you know what the result will be?

Your child is going to want to talk. Listening to you open up about your life and how you relate to the story will directly impact your child's urge to share and connect. You will find your child opening up about his or her own thoughts, understandings and connections to the story, and suddenly, you are having a conversation...

Reading, as I told you earlier, is infectious. It is infectious because it is thought-provoking, soul-stirring, reflective and redeeming, and things that touch us deeply like that make us want to talk. And when we start feeling the pull of what a good story does, most of the time what we end up talking about is *ourselves*.

TALK ABOUT THE STORY AND THE WORLD

There's one step further you will want to take in discussing your book together, and that is: how does this book connect with the world around you?

What world are we talking about? Well, all of them, really, but not necessarily all at once.

When kids are very small, their big world is *you* and any siblings. As they grow older, their world expands. It begins to include extended family, then their little friends, your neighborhood, their town. They begin to gain interest in the lives of strangers, of people across the country and, eventually, around the world.

We all have stories that we live every day. Learning to connect the stories that we read with not just our own stories but with the stories of others develops empathy and the ability to infer ("reading between the lines"), another critical skill your child needs to learn in order to become a great reader.

This applies to stories that are set in the past, the present and the future. Are you reading a historical fiction book about the enslavement of the Africans? Discuss the enslavement of others in our own day and age. Are you reading some science fiction about someone living on Mars? Discuss how we are working towards that goal today. Working your way through a story of a soldier in Iraq? You very well may know someone who fought or died in the Iraq War.

The goal? To use your reading together to expand your child's horizons.

Talking with you about what he or she reads is an integral part of your child developing the ability to not just recognize the plot or conflict of a story but to also understand the characters, understand themselves and understand the world around them. As was the case with me and my middle-school students, you may end up having a conversation about a book that changes their life.

Having that kind of experience is going to light a fire in your child's heart, and you, as the next practice shows, are going to need to tend it.

Practice #7: Feed the Fire

If there is one belief that I will forever hold regarding reading, it is this: *everyone* has the burning desire to read when they are young. And I mean EVERYONE.

The excitement that bubbles up in children when they realize that—after all these years of being read to—they are finally learning the skills that will allow them to read *on their own*? It's the most thrilling reality they have ever known. They realize that a new world is opening up to them, a world which they can explore *forever*. Suddenly, a mixture of curiosity and self-empowerment bursts into a veritable fireball in their souls!

And then...

We snuff it out.

There are so many, many ways we adults, both as parents and as teachers, kill the fire. Let's look at a few of them to make ourselves aware of what *not* to do. Then let's look at what we *can* do to feed that fire and keep it burning.

SNUFFING THE FIRE

Learning to read takes so much work. But our kids happily *want* to do the work until they are made to believe it isn't fulfilling or rewarding. We make them believe that their efforts are in vain.

I have no idea how it began, but reading, for many kids, has become a joyless competition or some mundane undertaking. For example, in school, kids are often required to keep a reading log or write a reflection after every single reading session, just so the teacher "knows" that the reading is being done. The problem? Suddenly the reading feels like a job instead of a joy.

How much actual value *is* there in keeping a reading log and tracking how many pages you've read that day? And is it not better to *discuss* a story with another person to gain a deeper understanding and another point-of-view instead of writing a reflection in a journal that no one can dialogue with?

My husband sheepishly admits to being a student who tended to *not* read the required books when he was in high school. But then the rest of the class would hold these fascinating, in-depth conversations about a story, and as he sat there listening, he suddenly had the burning desire to go read the book!

And then there is the testing. Teachers are required to constantly assess the "reading levels" of students using tests that are extremely subjective (I've given them). And the tests are often given in front of other students. The kids are then required to choose books from leveled collections. Students compare what level they are at to those of their classmates, and... you see where this is going?

Kids are shown, right from the start, that being "good" at reading means that you are one of the kids who reads at the highest "level." When we show kids that Smartie Susan is at Level K, and, oh–*you* are only at Level G...

And in social situations, parents talk about what "good readers" their kids are–or aren't.

HOW DOES THAT MAKE A KID FEEL? We've all experienced the defeat of "I'm-not-as-good-as-you." We all know how it feels. What does all this comparison do to the fire in that child's little soul? It either diminishes it or causes it to combust with arrogance. Neither one of those is a good thing.

Kids need to understand that we all learn differently, and that's okay. In fact, it's not just "okay;" it's science. It's part of what makes each one of us who we are, with our own interests, talents and personalities. What a dull world we'd live in if we all learned and were interested in and performed tasks the exact same way.

Different simply means different, not better. It is important that we reinforce this to ourselves and our kids, no matter what we parents hear from the media or what our kids hear at school. Each of our brains is unique. We each respond to different stimulation and exercises in our own unique way—which means we are going to learn different types of things at different speeds. You may pick up certain skills in reading faster than I do, but don't gloat! Sooner or later there will be something down the road that will be more difficult for you to learn.

STIR THE WEAK EMBERS

Regardless of the "level" of your child's reading ability, there will always be something for him or her to work on to become a better reader. Remember, reading is a skill that *must* be practiced and used continuously.

When you sit down to read with your child, have them read a page or two so you can listen to how they are reading. Pause and discuss with your child what you hear that is *good*: is he sounding out words correctly? Is she reading smoothly, even if a bit slowly? Is he putting some expression and feeling into what he is reading? Let your child hear their strengths.

Then pick one skill to work on for that day (or week!). Not sure of what that skill should be? Go back and take a look at the skills we discussed in Practice #5, and work on one of those. Maybe the skill you practice will be how to make the reading flow more smoothly. Maybe it will be thinking about the feelings that are expressed in the story and trying to show those feelings with your voice. Maybe it will simply be how to sound out a word (and if you are of a generation who wasn't taught phonics, get a workbook and *learn them* so you can help. And another tip? Always have a dictionary on hand. Practice looking up a word, and then use the pronunciation guide in the beginning of the book and beside each word to learn how to say it.).

Regardless of what skill you pick, remember: home is where happy reading happens! Don't harp or continually stop the story. You don't want to make this reading experience like school, nor do you want to frustrate your child with constant negative feedback. You simply want to periodically correct pronunciation as needed, model the skill you are working on, compliment quietly with a "Good job!" when he is successful, and then keep reading.

FEED THE FIRE

I grew up in a home where I was far from spoiled. I did not have toys or trinkets bought for me unless it was my birthday or Christmas. If I wanted something badly enough, I had to work and save my allowance to buy it with my own money.

Except when it came to books.

My parents were serious library-users. In fact, my mother used to tell us when we'd make our weekly library trip, "You can check out as many as you can carry." But my parents understood the thrill and value of *owning* a book, too. There really is nothing quite like carrying around a book that is yours, is there? And for kids, that thrill is ten times bigger than what you feel.

If you want to keep your child reading, keep the thrill alive and *get them books*.

Where should you go to acquire these books? I suggest hitting up thrift stores. Not only can you find books that are almost brand new, but you are also likely to discover some of your old favorites that you loved as a kid and are no longer in print. And children's books usually don't go for more than a dollar or two. You can walk out with a stack of books for the price of just one book bought at a big box bookstore.

But speaking of bookstores, there still is that thrill of walking into a store full of books...

And then there are library sales, if you aren't bothered by the labels and stamps.

And book swaps.

Craigslist.

Freecycle.

Yard sales.

Half.com.

And, yes, even Amazon.com.

The important thing is *keep the books coming in.* A fire must have kindling, and giving a child a new book is one of the best ways to stoke it.

You should have seen the kids' eyes light up when it was time for me to run the book fair at school. Their faces as they watched me wheel those big carts into the library? You would have thought it was Christmas. And for the week of school when the book fair was open for business? Every single one of those kids, whether they could buy a book or not, asked their teacher if they could come down to just look and touch the books and sneak a read.

Get your kids books. Use them to reward. Use them to surprise! Use them to learn about new things. Always be looking to feed that fire.

Which leads us to our next practice: kids grow. Interests change. PAY ATTENTION.

Practice #8: Pay Attention

It's stating the obvious to say that kids change. We all know they develop—not just physically but in their personalities, too.

But along with kids' changing personalities come changing interests, and this is something that we would be remiss to ignore.

I have a nephew who, for several years, was really into trains. Trains, trains, trains. Everything was trains. He ate, breathed and slept trains!

And then, one day—TITANIC! Everything was about the *Titanic*.

And now? It's World War II.

You know what his parents are doing? They are paying attention to their child and his interests. They are using their knowledge of their son to feed the fire burning within him. Thanks to them, you will not see him without a book on his favorite topic in his hands.

Let's talk about this "paying attention" thing, and then let's look at some ways that we can fuel this desire to read. We need to be conscious when our child shows interest in a new subject or a new movie coming out or possibly an all-too-embarrassing question that you as a parent just *won't* understand.

When children are young, they have this amazing hunger to learn about new things. The non-fiction section of my elementary school library was three times the size of my middle school library's non-fiction section. The biggest reason for that is when small children get into a topic, they want to read *everything* about it. I had more books on sharks in the library...and cats! And cars! And ghosts!

It's not that little kids don't love stories. They do. But there is something to that initial spark of realizing that "I-can-learn-about-*anything*-now" that translates into younger kids reading more non-fiction (books that are informational or tell true stories).

As kids get older, there is a shift. They start to read more fiction. That doesn't mean their specific interests are waning. They most definitely still have interests; they just seem to be more ready to read about them in a fictional setting. Pay attention to what your middle-grade child is drawn to or intrigued by, and start looking for good fiction that correlates to those interests.

For example, there is a lot of great historical fiction that deals with a real person or a historical event but builds several made-up characters into the story. If your child is interested in Bessie Coleman or the Salem witch trials or the tragedy of the *Titanic* or the discovery of King Tut's tomb, look for fiction books based around those topics, events or people. There's quite a bit out there.

Take advantage of your child's interests to learn more about the topic, too. You are never too old to learn, right? And acknowledging your own new learning will add to a good discussion.

Oh, the silver screen. There will always be a magic to it, won't there?

Then use it, for Pete's sake! Don't be afraid to wield its power! It's almost ridiculous how many books are turned into movies nowadays. Pay attention to what's coming out down the pike, research what books have already been made into movies, and you've got books lined up to read for months.

But there is one absolute requirement: read the book FIRST before you watch the movie.

Here's an example of why this is important: I read the book *The Outsiders* by S.E. Hinton with my sixth graders. We would read the book out loud together in class, all of us taking turns reading. We talked about it together, we cried about it together, and we closed the book together, wishing it would never end.

And then we watched the movie.

To all of you who never actually read the book and only watched the movie, I can hear you from here: "*The Outsiders* is the best movie ever!"

I am betting you are saying that because every single male hottie/tough-guy actor of the '80s was in the cast.

But you never read the book...

The truth about the movie?

NO COMPARISON to the book.

You should have heard the discussions in my classroom after the kids watched the film. They were *incensed*, fuming about how the story is changed in ridiculous ways and how it lacks the heart-wrenching depth of soul that explodes out of Hinton's book.

(On a side note, this is a book that your child is guaranteed to love. LOVE. I am not stretching the truth in any way when I tell you that *every single one* of my students over a six-year span—kids who said that they HATED reading—told me that they *loved* that book. Go get it.)

This is all to illustrate my recommendation of READ THE BOOK FIRST. Don't let a bad movie sway your child's amazing imagination and destroy the ability to create a character outside of an actor's face or a story that goes "against" the movie. Until your child is of driving age, you have control over the movie-going experience! Know and imagine and talk about the story with your own minds—*then* see what Hollywood does with it. Granted, you may be delightfully surprised once in a great while (*The Life of Pi*, may I suggest?). But most times, no.

Read the book, *then* watch the movie and see what great discussion will follow.

AND THEN THEY STOP TALKING

There are a few parents out there who will be fortunate enough to have a child who is open, trusting and willing to talk to you about almost anything. For the majority of parents, getting even a small glimpse into the ever-changing world of our adolescent child is not easy. When we do get one, I think "relief" would be the right word.

For most of us, our teenagers *don't* talk to us. It's pretty, darn typical, too (if you allow yourself to remember). They are going through changes with their bodies, their friends, their emotions, their parents (yes, *you* ARE changing, too, in how you interact and deal with them as a young adult). It's scary, it's confusing, and, from their perspective, "YOU JUST DON'T UNDERSTAND!"

Despite what we may *feel* those words mean, they really *don't* mean your child thinks she knows it all. It actually means that she knows she *doesn't* know it all and is too embarrassed to ask questions, because—well, the questions *are* scary and confusing and the thought that you (a parent who never appears to be confused, scared or unsure about much of *anything*) went through this, too? It just doesn't seem possible.

Respect your child's discomfort in approaching you for a full discussion. Let them know that you are always willing to talk to them; however, if they are more comfortable, they should feel free to get some books to help answer or deal with those difficult questions.

There are so many YA fiction books that deal with awkward topics. The days when books like *Are You There God? It's Me, Margaret* were considered shocking are long over. The world of teen books is openly addressing much more serious topics: divorce. Death. Sexuality and gender. Drugs and alcohol. Suicide. All kinds of abuse. The list goes on and on.

All topics you may find uncomfortable to talk about, too, huh?

A word of caution when looking for books that handle these awkward topics: some books out there may involve a particular topic but not be a constructive read. The writer is more into displaying the topic rather than dealing with the heart of the matter and helping a kid process their own questions about it. I recommend looking into the reviews of books and perusing those that have positive reviews from both adults and reading organizations. Finding the right book is important and can be an immense help.

A few thoughts on where to get these books: Books can be checked out at your local library, but your child might find this too embarrassing to do themselves. Fiction books might be less awkward for them, but if the books are non-fiction and informational in nature, you may want to do the checking-out for them or just purchase the books instead.

To help ease your teenager's embarrassment about having to interact with you about the books, you can always discreetly "hand off" the books you checked-out or bought by leaving them on your child's bed or on the desk in their room.

I also have a suggestion regarding the format: try e-books. They are discreet. They save your teenager from being self-conscious about holding up a book with "that-embarrassing-topic" displayed on the cover. Or just be prepared to have them reading in their room with the door closed a lot more than before.

Staying in tune with your child's evolving list of interests may be challenging, to be sure, but you may find yourself also intrigued. How many of your child's interests match your own? Or what about the opposite? What new things has your child taught *you* because they have interests different from yours? Add fuel to your child's fire by acknowledging to them when your reading on their interests taught you something new! There is great pride in learning you helped teach someone something that they never knew before.

Following interests adds variety, and variety is important. No one likes a stagnant world, especially when it comes to reading. Our next practice deals with how to keep things exciting and new—with genre!

Practice #9: Mix Things Up with Genre

When I took over my elementary and middle school libraries, the bookshelves were divided into three sections: fiction, non-fiction and reference.

Fiction books are not true (think the"f" in "fiction" stands for "false"). They are stories that are make-believe, pretend, made-up.

Non-fiction books are about true or real events, people, topics and ideas (think the "n.f." in "non-fiction" stands for "not false"). In a traditional library setting, poetry, classical literature, art and plays are also shelved in the non-fiction section.

Reference books are books that we refer to as collected places of very specific types of information, such as atlases, dictionaries and encyclopedias (even if the encyclopedia is only on one particular subject, like "automobiles").

This is how most "traditional" libraries are set up. The non-fiction books are generally arranged by topic, and those topics are categorized by that odd number on the spine called the "Dewey number," named after Melvil Dewey who created the shelving system.

While this system works well for public libraries, I didn't like how it worked for the kids at school. Just as you didn't use the card catalog very often as a kid, neither do students today. The explorative nature of children tends to have them do a lot of wandering around in the stacks (the bookshelves), and I decided that I as the librarian was going to use that instinct to the kids' best interest: I was going to separate the books largely (but not completely) by their genre—the *type* of book they were, so to speak, so that different kinds of books were easier to find. That way the kids knew where to go in the library based on what they were in the mood to read at the moment.

I tell you all this because as you are building your child's library, you may want to do something similar with your child's bookshelf. The informational non-fiction I left as it was, but I separated out all the other genres that were mixed into it. When dealing with the fiction books, I blended the different types of fiction (fantasy, action, mystery, drama, science fiction, etc.) together to allow for a broader browsing experience and simply organized all the fiction books by the author's name.

The important thing is to provide a variety of literature genres for your child to read. It is so easy to get stuck in a rut of something we like. I still have a hard time NOT eating chocolate peanut butter ice cream if it is available. Sometimes it takes someone suggesting (or straight up providing) something else for us to take a nibble—and find a new love. I used to lay a new book on my stepson's bed for him to find when he came home from school. Often times I'd later discover him reading it...

If you are new to building a library, you may be unsure as to what genres you should be looking for. No worries! I made a list for you with a description of what each one is all about. Let's take a look:

NARRATIVE NON-FICTION

This book genre is relatively new in its description. Is it non-fiction? Yes. But the style in which it is written is one that reads like a novel. It carries with it that "story-telling" feel of writing. I introduced them to the kids as "books that sound like a novel, but they are *true*." We discussed that everything written in these books *really* happened, even if it reads like something that was made-up. A book in this genre can be a biography or memoir of one particular person or animal; a narrative of a particular event; or perhaps the story behind a discovery or achievement. These books tend to be fascinating. They all may read like a made-up story, but they all really happened!

POETRY

Poetry tends to get painfully overlooked. When I would teach my poetry unit, I would start by asking the students, "How many of you hate poetry?" Almost every kid (including me) would raise their hand. Then I would ask them, "How many of you hate poetry because it tends to go something like this: 'Roses are red. Violets are blue...'" Again, almost all hands went up. We then would have a discussion about how a lot of us hate poetry because we've only ever heard stuff that is silly and doesn't mean anything of importance.

But then we would talk about the fact that there are some really special poems out there, poems that tell stories or make pictures in our minds of things that we deeply connect with. We then would spend the next number of weeks reading poems together, talking about them, illustrating them, sharing how they resonated with each of us. The kids would then choose a poem to memorize and recite in front of the class. It was always striking to me how many of them didn't choose funny poems and instead chose pieces that were reflective, lyrical or even downright sad. Some students would act out their poem as they recited it, not to be dramatic but because that's what good poetry does to us: it moves us.

And poetry isn't always squeezed into a few stanzas. There are also novels that are written in a poetic format called "free verse" (meaning there isn't necessarily a rhythm or rhyme to the words, but the writing flows in a beautiful way that prose typically does not). Look for these books. They often tell a story in a strikingly intimate and personal way from the main character's perspective.

Great poetry, by its very nature of being concise and succinct and largely pictorial, forces us to reflect on its layers of meaning and connect with the pictures that come to mind when we read it. Kids *can* do this. They are thinking and reflecting all the time. Sit and read Robert Frost with your child and then discuss what the poem is talking about. (Try "Stopping by Woods on a Snowy Evening" or "Mending Wall.") I think you'll be amazed at what your child can understand.

HISTORICAL FICTION

Historical fiction is pretty much what it sounds like. It is a story that is made-up but is centered around a particular person, time period or event in history. If your child is fascinated by anything historical, do some research and see what fiction has been written about it. Many times authors have a personal connection to the story, whether it is because they have ancestors who lived through a specific period or the writer grew up in a region where a famous event occurred. No matter the reason for its writing, historical fiction tends to be passionate about its subject, full of emotion and detail and thought-provoking discoveries that lead to plenty of intense discussion.

A fantastic bonus of historical fiction books? Because of the amount of research done to write them, the authors usually list their references in the back of the book. If your child really enjoyed the subject of the book, some of these references could potentially be future reading materials.

SCIENCE FICTION

This genre, also called "sci-fi," tends to be either loved or hated. It takes science and turns it on its head with big WHAT IFs: *What if* we could actually travel to Jupiter? *What if* we could move back and forth through time? *What if* nature really could communicate—and retaliate? The ensuing stories vary in their degree of plausibility and believability, but all usually play out some sort of moral or ethical lesson. Dystopian (futuristic "look-at-the-horrible-mess-we-are-in-because-we-made-this-bad-decision-as-a-people") literature generally falls into this genre, like *The Hunger Games* trilogy.

REALISTIC FICTION

Probably the most widely enjoyed genre, realistic fiction covers a wide range of sub-genres: action and adventure, drama, mystery, romance, comedy. What makes it so popular is the fact that these books are relatively believable. Their authors largely seek to model the stories after "real life" (even if plausibility is stretched *just* a bit). Books in this genre can be beneficial in helping kids explore and process some of the life issues mentioned in Practice #6.

FANTASY

Does your child like stories involving magic? Then stock up on fantasy books. Here is the genre of other worlds, of wizards and spells, of epic battles between good and evil. Made hugely popular in the middle of the last century by folks such as J.R.R. Tolkien with his *Lord of the Rings* trilogy and C.S. Lewis with his *Chronicles of Narnia*, myriad authors have created worlds beyond our own. Think of J.K. Rowling with the *Harry Potter* series. When discovered through the right book, this genre has a tendency to surprise readers with how well they like it.

ANIME

An old Japanese style of story-telling meaning "animated," anime tends to have almost a cult following. While you may know it for being an "animated" film or television show, anime originated in a drawn print format and is still widely produced both in Japan and around the world. Books are read from "back to front" and cover a broad range of genres themselves (usually fantasy, but also history, comedy, romance or a blend of genres). I will caution you: research anime carefully for age-appropriateness before you buy. There can be some rather racy images and subjects incorporated into some stories.

GRAPHIC NOVELS

This genre is rather new and rather misunderstood. Graphic

novels are *not*, no matter how they look to you, comic books. A comic book is written in short snippets and is, upon original definition, typically (but definitely not always) comical. The short, little excerpts tend to fit together to tell some type of story, as they are usually written in a serial format for publication, like the newspaper.

Graphic novels are also as their name describes. They are graphic in format (meaning "pictorial," NOT "explicit"), and they really *are* a full-length novel.

Many casual perusers of graphic novels (including many teachers) are fooled into thinking that these novels are "easy" to read because they consist mostly of pictures and the amount of text appears somewhat limited.

In actuality, the opposite is true of their complexity.

Graphic novels require not just a reading of the *words* but a very close reading of the *pictures* as well. Both need to be interpreted *together* to gain the full meaning of what is happening in the story. Due to the limited space, the text is usually written in a very concise and sometimes cryptic style, again forcing a very close and careful reading to interpret all that is being said. It's not an easy read, nor is it a quick one.

I beg you, if your child is attracted to graphic novels, *please* allow them to read them. It will do a world of good in advancing his or her reading skills.

REFERENCE BOOKS

You may be thinking that reference books are not something that we "read," in the usual sense, so there is no need to have them on your child's bookshelf. I am going to disagree. Learning to use reference books—especially dictionaries, encyclopedias and atlases—is a skill that is being lost to the generations. With this loss comes the loss of so much more:

- **learning etymology** – A dictionary tells what language a word originated from, when it originated, how exactly to pronounce the word, derivatives of the word, etc., etc., etc.
- **global and spatial awareness** – A large atlas provides so much more information than a tiny map on a screen: the location of countries in relationship to each other; how geography affects a country's people; the impact of one country on another; etc. Not to mention, where is that country the main character is living in, anyway?
- **the wonder** – Remember opening up a reference book intending to look up one subject and getting completely distracted by another and ending up learning so much more than you meant to? You might even have a kid who does this on purpose! My husband loved reading the Colliers encyclopedia when he was a kid, and I admit to getting distracted by the anatomy plates in our Encyclopædia Britannica as a middle schooler...

Definitely find copies of at least a good dictionary and a current atlas. Encyclopedias tend to be expensive, I know, but keep an eye out at library sales. They tend to renew their annual versions more frequently than anyone else. And check yard sales. Someone might be selling Grandma's old set.

AUDIO BOOKS

Do you remember in the old days when libraries had those little bagged sets of a book and a cassette tape, and you would go home and put the cassette tape in the tape player and read along in the book as the voice read to you (turning the page every time you heard the '*ding!*')?

They still have those–kind-of. Most libraries have a collection of audiobooks that are on CD or can be temporarily downloaded as a digital file onto your computer or smart device. Some school libraries also have what are called "Playaways," mini MP3 players downloaded with one book. Kids can check them out with the accompanying book and read along as they listen.

Audiobooks are a fantastic resource for anyone. Young kids to teenagers benefit from hearing yet another voice dramatize, express and pronounce words and bring a new story to life. And for those times when your child is *really* busy? Or when you are making that long road trip (and maybe your child gets sick when reading in the car)? These are great for "on-the-go" reading.

Check out Amazon/Audible for a great selection of downloadable audiobooks. You can usually purchase the corresponding book or e-book for a reasonable price.

MAGAZINES

This often-ignored little gem of literature is probably one of the simplest ways to keep your kids reading. Every month or two a brand-new issue is delivered right to their doorstep. Full of articles which provide great practice doing more "technical" reading, magazines are also quite inexpensive when purchased as a subscription. Or if you don't want to subscribe, check them out at the library! Many libraries even allow you to check out e-magazines for free, after you download a particular app.

CLASSICAL LITERATURE

I've saved this one for last (and, yes, intentionally put it in all caps) because I find this "genre" to be the absolutely most important.

Why?

Well, without getting into an opinionated argument of "classical literature is just *better*," I will say that, having read quite a few classics since early childhood (thanks to my parents), I can argue that these books generally have a few things going for them that most popular fiction typically does not:

- **solidarity**: These stories have stood the test of time through generation after generation of readers and continue to impact us today.
- **the complexity of language**: The writing style used a hundred plus years ago was definitely more advanced than is typically used today. This requires a more careful, thoughtful read which, in turn, develops a slower, more reflective read. There is simply more to take in and more for your brain to process. What does this mean? It means your young reader is diving to deeper levels of comprehension and connection in every classic he or she reads.
- **the vocabulary**: Words get phased out of use over time. Your child can learn so many "new" old words by reading the classics, significantly increasing their vocabulary and understanding of etymology.
- **the reference**: Classical literature—especially the Bible and ancient mythology—is referenced *all the time* in other works. If you don't know what Bible story or Greek god or

Shakespearean character a writer is referring to, you lack a foundation that helps you fully understanding the story. If you want to cheat and get abridged books that summarize the stories, fine. It would be better than nothing.

- **the history**: Want a good look at what times were like back in the "ol' days?" Pick up some classical literature. It will give you a very clear picture of a time period because it was written in that time! What better way to understand an issue than to read about it from a person who lived it! *Huckleberry Finn* by Mark Twain or Laura Ingalls Wilder's *Little House* series, anyone?

I cannot recommend strongly enough that you keep a steady supply of age-appropriate classics on hand to read with your child. Take them in slowly, talk about them and enjoy them. I promise you, you both will come to look forward to the depth of experience offered up by each of these amazing stories. One of my favorite reading memories is sitting and listening to my father read *The Swiss Family Robinson* to the family.

Even with such a large variety of genres to choose from, you will probably still find that your child goes through "waves" of liking one particular genre over the next. Don't worry. As with everything else, nothing lasts forever. And honestly? It doesn't *really* matter if they just really like science fiction and can't get enough of it. What matters is that your child is READING. Keep that as your primary concern.

Speaking of concerns, our last practice is the one that concerns me most, and once you learn about why, it will be your biggest concern, too. It is (gulp): SUMMER.

Practice #10: It's Summer! KEEP READING!

Oh, dear parents. As we come to the end of our journey together, it is here that I am going to give you the practice-to-end-all-practices. The one that, if need be, would have me on my knees with clasped hands, *begging* you to never forsake!

What is so important, you ask, that I am begging you to follow it without fail? Is it more important than keeping a bookshelf, reading together, and talking about what you've read?

It's not that it is more important. It's just that each practice plays such an integral role with all the other practices; they all work together. And this final practice is the tie that binds, so to speak. It keeps your child's growth continuously moving in a forward direction. It's the one that if you don't follow it, significant damage is going to be done to the progress your child has made over the school year.

The practice is this: **READ OVER THE SUMMER**.

Seriously? you might be thinking. *Can't my kids just give their brains a break? It's only twelve weeks!*

Yes, I'm serious. In fact, I could not be *more* serious.

Let's look at why this practice is so terribly important and what you need to do keep your child growing year-round.

THE RESEARCH

Believe it or not, for over 100 years researchers have been studying the negative effects of failing to read consistently over the summer (see the article by White under "Summer Reading" in the Supporting Resources). When school lets out, kids (and their parents!) tend to go into "recess" mode and take a break from practicing what they should be practicing most: reading! The consequences of taking the summer off are quite shocking, and they explain a lot about what we observe in schools. Let me get to the bones of what the research says:

When children do little to no reading for the two to three months of summer, their brain *forgets* about two to three months (or more) of learning.

This means that when these children return to school at the start of a new year, they have to scramble to *relearn* two to three months of previously learned knowledge. As new material is being introduced, their brains are still trying to catch up with the knowledge that has been forgotten, therefore not learning the new material and falling further and further behind.

And here's the worst part: this loss of learning and the months of schooling that it equates to is *cumulative*. The loss keeps building on itself, year after year. So if a third grade child has spent every summer staring at an iPad or computer, or maybe even running around in the yard–but not reading–their knowledge bank is most likely an entire YEAR behind their classmates. BY THIRD GRADE.

3 months NOT reading x 3 school years = 9 months LOST

That is ONE SCHOOL YEAR'S worth of knowledge lost!

This is why students who never read over the summer can be several years behind their fellow classmates by the time they reach high school, not to mention by the time they *finish* high school.

It is a serious problem, an injustice to kids that is largely inexcusable and avoidable.

Yes, I've said it: inexcusable and avoidable—now that you know.

So, summer rolls around. The family schedule that you've maintained for the past nine months is suddenly shot. Even if your child does attend summer school, most districts only run classes for half a day, so you still have a child with all this time on his hands. What do you do?

This spare time is a remarkable blessing! Instead of having to squeeze reading time into a schedule that is jam-packed with homework, school sports, community clubs and weekend activities, now your child has room to breathe and *read*. AND they can read whatever they want! There is nothing more liberating and joyful than freedom of CHOICE (and if your school district imposes a required summer reading list, argue against it. Kids need some time to truly read for enjoyment).

Let's consider some practical ways to incorporate reading into the summer so that you can curb this widespread problem from affecting your own child.

VACATIONS AND DAY TRIPS

Summer is a time when many people go on some sort of vacation or do a number of day excursions. Families tend to do trips that are geared around something educational: a museum, a national park, a monument, a city, a beach.

Why not do some reading about that city you are going to visit or about what you are going to see *before* you get there? Read about someone whose work you will see in a museum. Read about why that national park was set aside as a national treasure. Read about the event that led to that monument being placed in that specific spot. Read about the creatures that you will see on that beach.

I'm not talking reading on Wikipedia, either. I'm talking going to the library and finding books about that person, event, animal, city, whatever, checking those books out, and going home and learning all you can together about said topic.

Why?

So when your child actually sees this thing for *real* with his own two eyes, he will approach it with excitement because he now understands what makes it so special.

I grew up near Gettysburg, and we used to go to the Civil War museums all the time—something that as a pre-teen I thought was *totally* boring. Well, I will never forget one summer having some people stay at our house who had two boys my age. These boys were growing up in Japan, but being Americans, their parents made darn sure their boys knew American history. As I roamed the war museums with these boys, they told me story after story about the men and women that we saw depicted in the paintings and in the statues, and suddenly, I was fascinated. Suddenly these museums meant something. For the first time, I was excited to wander those dark halls full of stories.

Give your child that opportunity. Read to learn before you travel. Who knows? Your child may wind up teaching other vacationers standing around something new as they spout off information that you both learned together while you were reading.

Can't get to the reading before the vacation? Don't worry! If the opportunity doesn't present itself to read about a subject beforehand, you can also do it after! In fact, there is a whole different fascination with learning *more* about something that already whetted your appetite. Your child's memory of the trip may be the driving hunger behind continuing to research that person or event or city.

READING PROGRAMS

I don't know that I've ever known of a public library that didn't have a summer reading program. If you need some help structuring your child's summer reading, talk to the librarians in town. I can guarantee you they will have something going on for the local kids to keep them reading for the summer. It's more than likely, too, that your child will have friends who will be participating.

Many larger bookstores also have summer reading programs. Some offer incentives such as: if a child reads a specific number of books, journals about their favorite part of each story, and turns in the journal by a certain date, the child gets a free book!

FRIEND BOOK CLUBS

There are a good number of you who are part of a book club.

Why not have your child start one? Summer is the perfect time to spend lazy afternoons reading together with friends under a tree in the park or in a backyard. Depending on their age, parents might be able to join in, or kids can enjoy this time reading alone with their friends. Toss in a healthy snack to munch while they discuss, and you've got the perfect summer party. And, if there is a movie version of the book? Remember: BOOK FIRST! (And don't forget the popcorn.)

LITTLE FREE LIBRARY.ORG: TAKE A BOOK—RETURN A BOOK

Many of you have seen them: little birdhouse-looking boxes in people's yards or on street corners posted with a sign reading "Little Free Library." Inside the box are books. You are allowed to take a book out of that little "library" as long as you put a book back. Anyone can use it as many times as they want. Maybe you and your child can use the summer not only reading but making a Little Free Library of your own.

SCHOOL LIBRARIES

This option may not be available to you, and if it's not, I highly recommend that you and your other parent-friends talk to the school principal and school board about making it an option. That is: use the school library over the summer.

I worked in a school district where the public library was located in a part of town that was just *not* easy or safe to walk to. So how were the kids expected to get to the library to read if their parents worked and the kids couldn't walk there?

I spoke to my principal about it; I even had an aide of mine lined up who was willing to work in the library during the summer so the kids could have access to the books. Unfortunately, my principal was on her way out the door to a new job, and I was moving to a new state at the end of the school year. She said that it wasn't possible, and I didn't have any leverage to push it further.

But if I was a parent and a taxpayer, I'd push it.

Just saying.

YARD SALES

Summertime is the time for yard sales. You know what that means?

Yard sales = CHEAP BOOKS.

Twenty-five cent copy of *A Wrinkle in Time*, anyone?

Stock up, my friends. STOCK UP. And don't just look for books for now. Look for books for down the road. Your child is a developing reader. You are going to burn through books faster than you probably think you will. You've got a spare corner in the back of your closet for a stack of future reads, right?

My point is: you have *got* to keep your kid reading over the summer. Tell them why. When I had my end-of-the-year talk with my students about why it was so important that they read over the summer and showed them a pictograph of what happens when they don't, their eyes got as big as saucers. I then used that opportunity to hand each of them a new book purchased with the money made from the book fairs we had during the school year. You would have thought I handed each of them the moon. (See? Your book fair purchases really *do* help get books in the kids' hands!)

Share with your kids the dire consequences of failing to read over the summer. Get excited with them over the opportunity to read what they want. Go pick out your summer reads. And when that school bell rings that school's out? KEEP READING.

The Sum of the Practices

Well, here we are...at the end. But yet—for you—it's really just the beginning.

Like I said at the start of this book, I firmly believe that loving to read is a fundamental part of human nature. We as humans love to learn. That love never quits until it's smothered with other stuff. And I mean literally *stuff*. We as parents are to blame for that. We provide a lack of books but an excess of toys, video games and TV time—a lot of hours spent doing a whole lot of nothing productive.

Reading, on the other hand, is beyond productive. It is the one and only skill that is foundational to our children's success for the rest of their lives. It develops their brain, quite literally. It causes them to reflect. It builds their language skills. It forces them to think. It stretches them. It teaches them.

The only way your child will develop and grow and master that skill—the only way they will benefit from its life-changing effects—is to practice it every single day.

So go start that bookshelf. Get reading with your child. Tonight. Talk and connect over what you've read together.

Give your child the gift that will provide them a lifetime of success.

An Afterword

Dear Readers,

Regardless of how it may appear, writing and publishing your own work is an incredibly humbling experience. There were many, many times over the past months that I stopped and questioned myself about really having the "right" to write about this passion of mine: getting children to read.

But then I would start rereading my notes and drafts, and the fire would burst back into flame. I realized that I *had* to write this book. The hundreds of kids that I have worked with over the years—they are the ones who make me feel like I have something to say and, therefore, make me someone who has a "right" to say something. Those kids showed me the truth of the power of reading.

If this book has encouraged you and lit a fire in your heart, please share this book with others and leave a review online. I want the skills that I practiced as a teacher to guide *all* parents on their child's road to success.

And if you ever get discouraged and feel you are down to smoldering embers, skim back through this book to rekindle your fire. Parenting is not easy, I know. But the rewards of consistent structure, love, attention—and reading—will not go unrewarded. I promise you.

Rachael

Supporting Resources

Below are some additional books and articles related to topics that I touched on in this book. You may want to read through some of these resources for more information. Those that are marked with an asterisk (*) are more inspirational rather than technical in nature.

THE BRAIN:

Carter, Rita. *The Human Brain Book*. DK Publishing, 2014.

Stevens, Alison Pearce. "Learning rewires the brain." *Science News for Students*. Society for Science and the Public, 2 Sept. 2014. Web. 15 May 2018.

READING OUT LOUD AND READING TOGETHER:

Duursma, E, et al. "Reading Aloud to Children: the Evidence." *Archives of Disease in Childhood*, vol. 93, no. 7, 2008, pp. 554–557., doi:10.1136/adc.2006.106336.

Fox, Mem. *Reading Magic: Why Reading Aloud to Our Children Will Change Their Lives Forever*. Harcourt, 2008.

Goldstone, Lawrence, and Nancy Goldstone. *Deconstructing Penguins: Parents, Kids, and the Bond of Reading*. Ballantine Books, 2005.

Ozma, Alice. *The Reading Promise: My Father and the Books We Shared.* Grand Central Publishing, 2011.

Spufford, Francis. *The Child That Books Built: A Life in Reading.* Metropolitan Books, 2002.

Trelease, Jim. *The Read-Aloud Handbook.* Penguin Books, 2013.

Willingham, Daniel T. *Raising Kids Who Read: What Parents and Teachers Can Do.* Jossey-Bass, 2015.

SUMMER READING:

"Early Warning Confirmed: A Research Update on Third-Grade Reading." *The Annie E. Casey Foundation.* The Annie E. Casey Foundation, 29 Nov. 2013. Web. 15 May 2018.

McGill-Franzen, Anne, and Richard L. Allington. "Bridging the Summer Reading Gap." *Instructor*, May/June 2003.

White, W. "Reviews before and after vacation." *American Education*, 1906.

Suggested Reading Lists

I think it is important that you have some kind of reading list immediately available to you to add some kindling to the fire you are feeling right now about your child's success, so I have listed below some of my, my husband's and my students' favorite books that we have read and absolutely loved.

For a longer list of books sorted by genre, visit my "Suggested Book Reading Lists" board on Pinterest under the username "Reiton Publishing." Clicking on a book will take you to the corresponding book on Amazon where you can read its summary and reviews.

If you are interested in a best-seller list, you will find one that is updated every hour on Amazon.com.

BABY/TODDLER BOARD BOOKS:

A *Splendid Friend, Indeed* by Suzanne Bloom

The Going to Bed Book by Sandra Boynton

Goodnight Moon by Margaret Wise Brown, ill. by Clement Hurd

Vegetables in Underwear by Jared Chapman

Drummer Hoff by Barbara Emberley, ill. by Ed Emberley

Ten Little Fingers and Ten Little Toes by Mem Fox, ill. by Helen Oxenbury

An Alphabet by Oliver Jeffers

Let's Find Momo! by Andrew Knapp

Chugga-Chugga Choo-Choo by Kevin Lewis, ill. by Daniel Kirk

Not A Box by Antoinette Portis

PICTURE BOOKS:

Corduroy by Don Freeman

Mother Bruce by Ryan T. Higgins

Actual Size by Steve Jenkins

The Snowy Day by Ezra Jack Keats

The Story of Ferdinand by Munro Leaf, ill. by Robert Lawson

The Lion and the Mouse by Jerry Pinkney

A *Sick Day for Amos McGee* by Philip C. Stead, ill. by Erin E. Stead

Alexander and the Terrible, Horrible, No Good, Very Bad Day by Judith Viorst, ill. by Ray Cruz

Knuffle Bunny by Mo Willems

Owl Moon by Jane Yolen, ill. by John Schoenherr

EARLY READERS:

Hi! Fly Guy by Tedd Arnold

Go, Dog, Go! by P. D. Eastman

Drop It, Rocket by Tad Hills

Danny and the Dinosaur by Syd Hoff

Harold and the Purple Crayon by Crockett Johnson

Frog and Toad Are Friends by Arnold Lobel

Little Bear by Else Holmelund Minarik, ill. by Maurice Sendak

Hand, Hand, Fingers, Thumb by Al Perkins, ill. by Eric Gurney

Green Eggs and Ham by Dr. Seuss

Caps for Sale: A Tale of a Peddler, Some Monkeys and Their Monkey Business by Esphyr Slobodkina

EARLY CHAPTER BOOK SERIES:

Ivy & Bean series by Annie Barrows, ill. by Sophie Blackall

Rabbit & Robot series by Cece Bell

Flat Stanley series by Jeff Brown, ill. by Macky Pamintuan

Zoey and Sassafras series by Asia Citro, ill. by Marion Lindsay

Mercy Watson series by Kate DiCamillo, ill. by Chris Van Dusen

Judy Moody series by Megan McDonald, ill. by Peter H. Reynolds

Stink series by Megan McDonald, ill. by Peter H. Reynolds

The Magic Tree House series by Mary Pope Osborne, ill. by Sal Murdocca

Big Nate series by Lincoln Peirce

Lulu series by Judith Viorst, ill. by Lane Smith

MIDDLE GRADE BOOKS:

Tangerine by Edward Bloor

Walk Two Moons by Sharon Creech

Catherine, Called Birdy by Karen Cushman

The Outsiders by S. E. Hinton

Snow Treasure by Marie McSwigan

Island of the Blue Dolphins by Scott O'Dell

Where the Red Fern Grows by Wilson Rawls

Paperboy by Vince Vawter

"The Sword in the Stone" from *The Once and Future King* by T. H. White

Feathers by Jacqueline Woodson

YOUNG ADULT BOOKS:

Speak by Laurie Anderson

Ironman by Chris Crutcher

The Count of Monte Cristo by Alexandre Dumas

Lord of the Flies by William Golding

The Life of Pi by Yann Martel

Monster by Walter Dean Myers

Boy21 by Matthew Quick

Dracula by Bram Stoker

Code Name Verity by Elizabeth Wein

The Book Thief by Markus Zusak

SERIES BOOKS (IN ORDER OF DIFFICULTY):

Joey Pigza series by Jack Gantos

The Chronicles of Narnia by C. S. Lewis

A Series of Unfortunate Events by Lemony Snicket, ill. by Brett Helquist

Hatchet series by Gary Paulsen

Redwall series by Brian Jacques

The Face on the Milk Carton (Janie Johnson) series by Caroline B. Cooney

The Giver Quartet by Lois Lowry

Iron Druid Chronicles by Kevin Hearne

Anne of Green Gables series by L. M. Montgomery

The Lord of the Rings by J. R. R. Tolkien

ADULT BOOKS SUITABLE FOR OLDER KIDS:

Jurassic Park by Michael Crichton

The Boston Girl by Anita Diamant

All the Light We Cannot See by Anthony Doerr

James Bond Series by Ian Fleming

Abraham Lincoln: Vampire Hunter by Seth Grahame-Smith

Cat and Mouse by Günter Grass

A Prayer for Owen Meany by John Irving

Devil in the White City by Erik Larson

Lonesome Dove by Larry McMurtry

Aubrey/Maturin series by Patrick O'Brian

A Thousand Thanks

Having the burning desire to write a book is one thing. Actually turning it into a reality and publishing it on your own is a whole other thing. I could not have completed this book without the following individuals and the amount of support they gave me.

First, I want to recognize my parents and sibs for their hidden editing talents and crazy encouragement. You guys have no idea what all your work and book love has meant to me. I love you guys so fricking much.

To my U.F.; my mother-in-law, Barb; my "sista" Brenda; and my "little cuz," Molly: thank you for taking the time to read what you could and giving me the love and emotional support when I needed it!

To Mr. Fisher: the discussion we had together years ago was unconsciously about this book. Thank you for making me see the value in what I was feeling and what I had to say.

To my slew of friends who are gut-bustingly honest, insanely patient and immensely supportive—thank you for taking the time to read through this whole thing and giving me your very sage advice and excellent suggestions: Cherie, Erika, Judene, Kat, Mark, Marie, Nik, Paula and Richard. I don't know what I would do without you guys. Seriously.

To Liz: this manuscript would still be sitting on my desk if not for you. Thank you for taking me, this book and our friendship so seriously.

To my dear stepkids, Michael and Hannah: this is all for you, too. I hope it inspires you to go out and do what you feel passionate about. I love you both so *$!%# much.

To my husband, Derrick... Words cannot express my gratitude for all you've given me, including the opportunity to write this book. If only the world were filled with husbands as generous and loving as you.

And finally, to every single one of my students: you are the reason this book exists. Reading, as we all experienced together, is an emotional business. Thank you for trusting me with your hearts. Don't ever give up on what we learned together. And if you've stopped reading, email me. I'll give you a couple good titles to get you back on track, and maybe we can read them together...

Helpful Pinterest Boards

Here are a couple links to Pinterest boards I put together that you may find helpful in the building of your library:

Bookshelf Ideas:

https://www.pinterest.com/reitonpublishing/bookshelf-ideas/

Recommended Reading Lists:

https://www.pinterest.com/reitonpublishing/recommended-reading-lists/

Other Books by Rachael T. Reiton:

Marley Eats His Vegetables

Marley the big dog loves squirrels and people food (especially sugary, sweet, people food). One day, quite by accident, Marley discovers he loves VEGETABLES! Illustrated with photographs of the author's dog, Marley will certainly make you and your kids laugh—and just may get the kids to eat their veggies! A book for young readers.

Available as an ebook on Amazon.com or in print at http://www.blurb.com/b/7854737-marley-eats-his-vegetables.

Made in the USA
Middletown, DE
06 July 2018